Help, my dog's on Twitter
(A dogs guide to Twitter & life in general)

Harry the Spaniel

Copyright © 2012 Harry the Spaniel

All rights reserved.

ISBN: 1480211850
ISBN-13: 9781480211858

DEDICATION

Dedicated to my hooman pawents (Boss mum Heather and Second in command mama Yvonne), sisfur Madmaggiemoo, Hooman Gwanny and all my anipals on Twitter especially Summer & Stan, Angel the Furball, Dog Murray, Humf, Auntie Gillibean, Uncle Sandy, Bestest Gun Dog, Harv the Tibetan, Mrs C, Monty, The eejits and all the others who make me laugh every day.

CONTENTS

Acknowledgments

Foreword

1	Twitter – de puppy stage	Pg1
2	Finding wuv on Twitter	Pg 4
3	What my pals has to say	Pg 8
4	A typical day or two	Pg 34
5	Tennis Balls – My Experiences	Pg 43
6	It wasn't me	Pg 46
7	My last thoughts	Pg 50
8	Dictionary fur hoomans	Pg 51

ACKNOWLEDGMENTS FROM THE CO-AUTHOR HEATHER NESBITT HARRY'S MUM

I would like to express my gratitude to Harry and Maggie who have lit up not only my life but those of people and animals they interact with. Without Harry and his unique personality this book would never have been possible.

Harry started on Twitter when I was seriously ill and the dogs he has interacted with over the last months have greatly lifted my spirits so I thank you all from the bottom of my heart.

Thank you to my partner Yvonne and my mum Ellie for listening to me read out the various tweets that Harry and Maggie have received.

Last and not least thank you Twitter for having such a vehicle available that we can express ourselves on so freely.

FOREWORD

My name is Harry I am an English Springer Spaniel and I am vewy vewy handsome BOL (bark out loud) I live wiv my hoomans and my sisfur Maggie and I wuv dem vewy much. You will have noticed dat dogs have der own language when typing. To help de hooman weaders I have done a dictionary at de back of my book to makes it easier fur yoo to twanslate. I is fought full like dat!

Dis book is about my experiences on Twitter and life in general wiv all my pals and some vewy wuvly hoomans too. Some of my pals has been kind enuff to let me do interviews wiv dem which are funny and sad.

I hope it makes u howl wiv laughter and no cwy too much as I has had great fun in writing it.

1

Twitter – de puppy stage

So you decided to take de plunge and joined Twitter. Where does you start? After all it is a dog eat dog world out der! BOL

Twitter is a big world wiv lots of wuvly hoomans and anipals but also not so nice hoomans too! Grrrrrr! My dog advice to you is avoids eggs! Eggs are hoomans who won't put der picfurs up of demselves. I also has had pwoblems wiv twitter hoomans who has naked photos of demselves........YUK.

Some stoopid hoomans also ask you questions on twitter which is ok but dey ask you as if you too are hooman which you clearly is not if you is a dog or cat or hamster! I has been asked "Do you know what is in your food?" My response to a question like dat is "I is a dog I is not hooman I does not wead vewy well so I not know what in my food" or "I is a dog I eat anyfing and does not take much interest what is on de packet" BOL dat normally stops dem askin again.

So, in order to assist you through your first pawsteps I has listed some fings dat you may come across dat may confoos you. I has also listed some suitable wesponses on de next pages.

1) *"Hey no judgements but do you really know what is in your pet food?"*

I have given you two responses to dat above but here is anofur one, "My Mum does. Can I smell your bum"

2) *"You see this video of someone taping you?"*

Nefur efur efur open de link attached to a message like dis as it will mess up your twitter account and possibly your IBone or IPawd or your compooter. Dis is a stooped hooman twyin to harm you so jus ignore dem like it is your hoomans given you a tablet.

3) *"Would you like some followers? Follow me and I will get 20,000 followers for you"*

Again dis is a norty hooman twyin to do you harm (I want to bite der arses) Why you need 20,000 followers? Dat is lots of bums to have to sniff to make introductions. Dat a waste of your time and sniffs. Ignore dem pwonto.

4) *"someone is spreading nasty photos about you on twitter"*

Dis again is a stoopid hooman who wants you to click a norty link. Don't do it no-one is spweading any photos of you wivout you knowing we is anipals we would let you know first BOL.

As well as stoopid hoomans tweeting you messages twyin to catch you out (as if, you is a dog you is far more intelligent dan dem) der are a few ofur things that wills help you along de way.

1) Have a photo of yourself to show you is real.

2) Be polite but you can also be norty and cheeky too and get away wiv it!

3) If a doggie or nice hooman follows you (or any ofur anipal) follow dem back dat way you will make lots of fweinds and have much more fun.

4) Join in de conversations you will not make many fweinds if you is silent.

5) Don't growl at de ofur types of anipals on twitter like de cats or de hamsters. Dey are your fweinds we wespect dem. Surpress your urges.

6) If you is a dog you should alweady be familiar wiv de language used on twitter by de ofur dogs. However keep dis book to paw so you can wefer to the dictionary at de back in times of need.

7) You can be cheeky about your hoomans on twitter. De ofur anipals will finds it funny and agwee wiv you. I talked about stealing my mums pink knickers de ofur day and lots of ofur dogs said dey stole der mums knickers too BOL.

8) You will soon realise dat bein on twitter will confirm how normal you weally is and it is your hoomans dat are stwange BOL.

9) Airing your gweivances on twitter about your hoomans and just how dim dey are will makes you feel better about yourself.

10) You can pwactice your sad face on twitter by posting your photos of you pwactising. Ofur dogs will score you. Dis will ensure dat you get it right fur when you needs to use it and mean you get what you want first time.

Above all in de early stages be fweindly and make fweinds. If you knows someone on twitter follow der lead (pardon de pun) I is on twitter you can always follow me or my pals and we will see you right.

2

FINDING WUV ON TWITTER

I am vewy lucky to have found de wuv of my life on Twitter. Ofur dogs has not bin so lucky as me including my own sisfur Maggie (@madmaggiemoo)

Maggie has had her heart bwoken twice now but bein a dog she is quite resilient and her bwoken heart lasts minutes not days and is often healed wiv de help of some kind of tweat and a walk on de field! BOL

Dis is my sisfur Maggie here

I fink she is bootiful even if she does insist on hanging fwom my ears at efury opportunity!

So back to de wuv of my life. I has a best mate on twitter called Stan we bin pals fur a while now and I fink he is fab. Now I found out a few months ago dat Stan had a sisfur called Summer and I had seen a picfur of her and she is bootiful and gawgus. Summer did not have her own Twitter account and Stan was getting quite cheesed orf passing messages between us. He is no cupid I tell you dat!

Eventually Summer got her own account and our wuv started to blossom fwom der. In order to woo Summer I sings to her and has now been called de #crooningcanine by ofur dogs on Twitter. I also gets requests. To shows you what I means below is one of de songs I has wooed Summer wiv;

I wuv u jus de way u are

Don't go changing to twy & please me
U nefur lets me down befur
Don't imagine u too familiar &
I don'ts see u anymore

I wouldn't weave u in times of twouble
We nefur coulds has come dis fur
I tooks de good times I takes de bad times
I takes u jus de way ur are.

Don't go tryin some new fahion
Don't change de colour of ur fur
U always has my unspoken passion
Although I might not seem to care
I don'ts want clever confursation
I nefur wants to work dat hard
I jus want someone dat I can talk to
I want u jus de way u are

I needs to know dat u will always be
De same old someone dat I knew
What will it take fur u to believe in me
De way dat I believe in you

I woofed I wuv u and dats forever
& dis I pwomise fwom de heart
I could not wuv u any betfur
I wuv you jus de way u are.

Dis is de wuv of my life Summer known as Harrys Girl;

Yoo too could find wuv on Twitter if you paw your cards right. Jus follow my simple wules below;

1) Don't rush in like we normally does as dogs. Takes it slow and steady likes u is stalkin a spider.

2) It is normal fur you as a dog to sniff bums dat does nots mean dat if someone sniffs ur bum dey want to date u.

3) Ofur dogs on Twitter will tease you fur havin a

girlfweind/boyfweind do not rise to de bait jus ignore dem dey is losers (though sometimes dey is ur pals and dat kinds of teasing is ok)

4) Do not get distracted by ofur dogs unless u has agweed wiv ur girlfweind/boyfweind dat you can play de field. Dis leads (pardon de pun) to confoosion and annoyance and lots of barking and howling which is vewy annoying.

5) Interbweed welationships is acceptable on Twitter.

6) Do not be afwaid to show ur emotions wiv ur wuv you can also share your treats too wivout growling or nuffin like dat as it is wude.

7) Enjoy ur Twitter wuv and don't furget to plan lots of dates and BOL.

3

WHAT MY PALS HAS TO SAY

I has some gweat pals on Twitter and we has gweat fun wiv eachofur nearly every day. I asked some of dem to do an intervoo wiv me and here is de wesult!!!

Summer
@SummerHollett

She is a German Shepherd Dog and is de wuv of my life.

1. Hi Summer my wuv how's u doin?

"Hallo, my dawlin - I's fine thank you. I's been knitting some socks for your little naked legs after your hoperations. I miss you lots."

2. How old is yoo?

"I think I'm about six now. Mum and dad adopted me last year from a very nice lady in Derby. She never puts a healthy dog to sleep, but my last owners were thinking of doing that cos I was too boysterwus for dem. I've lost lots of weight and luvs to wun and wun and wun now and I'm so lucky to live with Stan and mum and dad that I's not bothered that I don't weally know how old I am."

3. Why did you choose me to be ur boyfweind?

"It was wuv at first sight - Stan showed me a picture of your bad hair day foto and I fell for you der and den."

4. What does u wuv most about me?

"You have a bootiful face and I wuvs your sense of hoomor: you makes me larf soooo much. You is like Stan: you can't help getting into twubble, but you don't mean to be nawty."

5. Why did u join Twitter?

"So that I cuds talk to you instead of getting Stan to givs you messages"

6. What does u enjoy most about bein on Twitter?

"Being Hawwy's Girl and haffing you sings to me. I've met some wufferly dogs on Twitter, but it's not de same when ur not about."

7. Does u fink Twitter is a good fing fur dogs and hoomins if so why?

"Yes, I fink it's good. We dogs can share things like what

foods are good or bad for each ofur and get to learn what ofur dogs do wif der owners. I know that Stan was pleased when he found out that other dogs nicked underwear: he's just got to learn to avoid the door now so he can make a clean get away."

8. Does u tweet wiv any ofur anipals on Twitter is yes what kind?

"Not weally - can't follow any cats or wabbits as they has to be chased."

9. Does u fink dat wuv on Twitter can weally work?

"I fink dat we're liffing proof dat it can work - and maybe our mums will be able to do some business togefur in de footure as well!"

10. How much does u wuv me?

"I'd give you my last Dentastix! (well, maybe half of it!! BOL)"

Angel de Furball
@angelthefurball

She might be small but she can bweak anyfing in her way. She is part of de Crooning Canine Group!

1. Hi Angel how's u doin?

"Well Harry to be honest I am feeling a little naked since my haircut, being a furless furball is a little embarrassing, but apart from that all is good."

2. How old is u?

"Well because I was a street scruff my age is approximate, but we think me is 7 years old, however due to my silly brain being stuck in puppy mode I think I am 7 months, and most people think I am a puppy when they first meet me because way me acts and walks."

3. Does u have any brofurs or sisfurs?

"No brofurs or sisfurs but I does have lots of crazy hooman cousins who help me in my mischief making and sneak me little treats."

4. Who does u live wiv?

"I lives with me hooman slaves, I has tried to train them the best a furball can but as you know Harry it is not easy. I still cannot get them to understand you do your toilet outside. Any advice in this delicate matter would be appreciated."

5. U wecently started to play an instrument on twitter when I was singing what ofur instruments does u play?

"Well Harry, you may not know but I also plays the piano and I can jump on them Scottish bagpipes and make a terrible noise. I also occasionally plays my hooman cousins drums with my whip like tale."

6. Does u enjoy bein part of de Crooning Canine group?

"Oh yes, me is delighted to be part of the Crooning Canine Group, I looks forward to seeing the Cats Choir faces when we beats them to the coveted Christmas No 1 slot. The fur will surely fly."

7. U is a special dog wiv a special walk what happened to yoo?

"Well I was found in the street with head and spine injuries and showing the classic signs of having been abused. As all the damage to my brain occurred when I was a pup, me is now stuck in puppy mode and acts silly. I also takes little fits and was adopted by a few different people who returned me to the home saying me was too much work, but really me just

needs little help now and then. Because of me neurological and spinal damage me walks in me own special way, some people call me the dancing dog, others calls me the drunk dog but me hoomans just calls me the special dog. I cannot go up or down stairs on my own but me has a hooman chair lift so it not a problem."

8. What does u enjoy most about bein on Twitter?

"Meeting all you anipals and hearing the mischief you gets up to. I also enjoys tweeting silly pictures of myself and is proud of the fact that I has hundreds more followers than me hoomans."

9. Does u fink Twitter is a good fing fur dogs if so why?

"Yes I thinks it is good thing as we needs somewhere to discuss hooman behaviour, what is normal, what is not. I have learned much and am now aware that my hoomans are not normal but I is keeping them anyway."

Humf
@humfthecocker

He is a Cocker Spaniel wiv a musical flare. He is part of de Crooning Canine Group.

1. Hi Humf how's u doin?

"Hey Hawwy pal, me is doing great fanks. Me just been out wiv da dog walker and me furiends. Me did ave a swim so came back soggy. Mum moaned as usual bol!!"

2. How old is u?

"Me does be 2 years and err.....8 monfs old."

3. Does u have any brofurs or sisfurs?

"In me litter dere was 6 of us. I sometime see me biological sisfur Fudge, out on me walkies. We looks nearly identical, cept me is da cuter one obviously"

4. Who does u live wiv?

"Me does live wiv me Mum. She does be old.....errrrr 34. Bol"

5. How long has u bin playin musical instruments?

"Me likes to sing (Mum calls it howling like a banshee...not sure wot dat means) since me was little, then me took up armonica, guitar and peeano."

6. Does u enjoy bein part of de Crooning Canine group?

"Yeah it's great fun!!! I love your crooning Hawwy and we all gets on so it does be fab."

7. Why did u join Twitter?

"Me Mum was on Twitter for a few monfs before me, den I kept pestering er to let me ave me own account. Me wanted to talk to other anipals and share pics of me cute self. I now got more followers dan er, more dan 800 now!!!! Wows"

8. What does u enjoy most about bein on Twitter?

"Well me met me beautiful basset hound girlfriend on Twitter. Er name is Dupee and she does be me soulmate. She lives in Alabama USA so it do be a long distance relashunship, but we makes it work. She makes me soooooo happy and waggy tailed. Me also loves being on Twitter cos I get to make furiends all over da world and the fun we have is awesome. I have many BFF's on here. We always do be bol!!!!"

9. Does u fink Twitter is a good fing fur dogs if so why?

"Oh it's def a great thing, as well as fun our humans can gets advice and tips from fellow dog owning humans about our health and behaviour and boring stuff. It's also great to see pics of all different bweeds. If you are a dog or a human owner of a dog weading dis, I highly recommend joining Twitter now!!! Go on.....huwwy up and follow"

Auntie Bean
@gilliana09

She is a hoomin and makes powidge fur us dogs when she wemembers! She had a bootiful doggy called Brie hoo is in de picfur above.

1. Hi Auntie Bean how's u doin?

"Hi Harry, I'm fine thanks and thank you for being such a polite young man and asking. I hope you're okay too and that your leg is healing nicely."

2. Is yoo young or old in dog years?

"In dog years I think that I'm about middle aged-ish... about 6 and a bit years old which means I'm also middle aged in human years too. I don't feel my age and I know that I don't act my age, but you see I plan to grow old very disgracefully!"

3. Yoo used to have a bootiful dog would she have wuved Twitter too?

"My beautiful girly dog was an English Springer Spaniel called Brie (she had lots of nicknames too) and she would have loved Twitter – she did have own email account but didn't get around to setting up a Twitter account as she was always too busy being a span... oh and being cute, cuddly, cheeky, sweet and sleeping (she snored quite loudly for a lady... I have recordings of her!)"

4. Who does u live wiv?

"I live with my husband, Brie's Hudad... He's on Twitter too."

5. Why did u join Twitter?

"I joined Twitter originally to see what all the fuss was about, but initially I didn't 'get it', but then I read an article about @StephenFry - a person whom I admire very much – about how he had lots and lots of followers but he had stopped using Twitter because some people were being unkind and rude toward him... I don't like it when people are upset by others or made to feel uncomfortable, sad or unhappy. Well I decided to follow him so that I could voice my support and it kinda took off from there so to speak."

6. What does u enjoy most about bein on Twitter?

"I love Twitter because I've 'met' lots of lovely Tweeple, and of course lots of lovely furry Tweeters too. I don't really actually 'know' many of the Tweeters who I follow or who follow me, but we have such good fun and sometimes the Tweets can be helpful and informative too. Twitter gives folk a chance to catch up with events be they life changing or mundane and I think that it helps to put things

into perspective – y'know like if you're having a bad day then there's a balance of Tweets to help you see that there's always someone who's worse off than yourself and could do with your moral support just to let them know that somewhere, someone is sending them positive thoughts and support and a whole heap of Tweets that make you smile, laugh out loud and just plain make you feel better about things. Sometimes I get a little lonely or down when I'm by myself working, but I know that when I have a tea break or my lunch, my pals on Twitter will cheer me up with a kind word, a cute picture or just by regaling their followers with details of their exploits – from the humdrum, everyday trials and tribulations to the triumphs, adventures and happiness of muddy puddles, wet dog odours (eau de wetdog for the uninitiated), puppies and noms! I love it all. Twitter keeps it real... I don't like trolls, cyber-bullies, spammers or pornbots though they are just nasty, annoying and rude!"

7. Does u fink Twitter is a good fing fur dogs and hoomins if so why?

"Twitter can be good for dogs, humans... well everybody really so long as we all get along and everyone is nice not naughty (remember! Santa sees everything!) and we all enjoy the opportunity to 'speak' that has been given to us and use it wisely for the right reasons."

8. Does u tweet wiv any ofur anipals on Twitter is yes what kind?

"I think I mainly Tweet with dogs and their humans, some humans that have dogs and a few other humans... Ooh, I've just had a quick look through my list of followers and followees (is that even a word or have I just made a new word up?) and I think there may be a couple of cats in there too..."

Well Harry, that's all the interview questions done. Thanks for interviewing me, you'd make a great reporter – a proper news hound! (#literaryspan), but to me you will always be my brave, funny, handsome furry pal and #crooningcanine

Bye for now *sends lots of Gilli hugs and lug fusses* REMEMBER!! #spansrule

Murray
@Dog_Murray

He is a Cocker Spaniel and is vewy special. He can be funny and sensible too! Not sure how dat work.

1. Hi Murray how's u doin?

"Harry me pal I iz doing good today!!.... da vets finally think dey MIGHT have me meds right.... you know how hard it has been for mum to be seeing me doing the fitting and I don't like getting her upset and sad cos I love her so much so we is all hoping that things might start getting better although I iz not cured... but at least I can concentrate on making messes and having fun!"

2. How old is u?

"I iz 1 me barkday is the 14th July"

3. Does u have any brofurs or sisfurs?

"Yeah I have a older sisfur – Nala Cat she is a black puddy and is very sweet but boring! doesn't like playing with me and my toys but sometimes we have a cuddle...think she more interested in my twitter pals! she stole my account to start messaging my pal cabs and now they is a couple!"

4. Who does u live wiv?

"I lives wiv me mum and Nala Cat... but I stay at my granny's and grandpaw's at least once a week too! its really fun there! grandpaw does a gravy bone hunt in da garden!!"

5. Why did u join Twitter

"Mum said I could join cos she seen other doggies on dere and thought it would be fun for me to see if others have epilepsy too so we knows we arent on our own"

6. What does u enjoy most about bein on Twitter?

"I love chatting with my best pals and sharing photos!

And when i have been ill dey all been very supportive and keeping dere paws crossed for me to be getting better. It makes me feel so lucky to know that people care and want me to be driving mum crazy with me mess, destruction and cuddles and not with me fits."

7. Does u fink Twitter is a good fing fur dogs if so why?

"Of course it is a good thing!! we can have fun and chat about all da cool things and when our mums and dad drive us nuts other dogs understand....mum always drive me

mad making me watch silly programs like x factor to check out the boys!! my pal humf's mum does da same so we laugh at them! Me Mum and Humf mum are cockermumtwins! I also met me love Katy xxx"

8.   Does u tweet wiv any ofur anipals on Twitter is yes what kind?

"just some cats...my best cat pal Cabs is Nala's boyfur...."

Stan de man
@stanleyhollett

He is my pal and brofur of Summer he is a knicker stealer too.

1.   Hi Stan de Man how's u doin?

"Hi, Harry - I's fine. How's you after your operations? Summer been very concerned about you and your shaved legs and has been knitting socks for you like crazy!"

2.   How old is yoo?

"I is 2 ½ years old - mum says I really should start to be a bit more grown up now, but I think she's boring!"

3.   Does yoo mind me and your sisfur dating?

"I don't mind at all, except that since she became so

besotted with you, she hogs the phones all the time and I don't get to tweet so much."

4. Who does u live wiv?

"I live with Summer, who came to live with us last summer (2011, mum says) and my mum and dad. Mum and dad have had me from when I was 10 weeks old and mum has trained me. She says I am getting a bit calmer as I get older, but I love to play and act the fool, but specially I love cuddles with my mum. I am very privileged as mum and dad don't usually buy puppies, they have always had dogs from rescue homes before."

5. Why did u join Twitter?

"Hm, good question. Mum is on Twitter as well, but she didn't really enjoy it so she had the idea for me to have a look for other German Shepherds to exchange ideas, experiences and stuff so I could see that I wasn't being hard done by in my training regime! Ironic that I'm now best mates with more spanners than GSDs!"

6. What does u enjoy most about bein on Twitter?

"Hearing how other dogs live and what their hoomans do with them and knowing that nicking mum's underwear from the washing basket is a normal thing for a boy to do! I don't like things that are too serious."

7. Does u fink Twitter is a good fing fur dogs and hoomins if so why?

"I think it's good if used properly - dad gets a bit grumpy if we spend too long on it, but it's just a bit of fun. I love hearing what other dogs get up to and I also follow some working dogs and it's great to learn what they are not

allowed to do or are allowed to do that's different to what me and Summer learn. Like, police dogs aren't allowed to open doors by themselves, but I can let myself into the bathroom if she hasn't bolted the door properly! She's training me to close doors behind me now, but so far there doesn't appear to be enough chilli sausage in the supermarket. She says I'm just being stubborn as I'm not a dumb dog! I think it could be good as well as my mum and your mum are talking about meeting up in person, so it's good for them too."

8. Does u tweet wiv any ofur anipals on Twitter is yes what kind?

"No, just dogs really - think I have some cat followers, but I tend not to follow cats as I have to chase them when they move - just can't help myself! I tweet with some hoomans as well who would like to have pets, but can't for some reason. Think they must miss their animals very much."

Gunner
@bestestgundog

Her indoors calls him The Bestest Gundog in the world. He's a workin spwinger spanl and he weally wuvs his job!

1. Hi Gunner how's u doin?

"I'm doin' very well Harry; don't think I ever had a day when I wasn't doin well..."

2. How old is yoo?

"I was born on 8th March 2007 so She Who Must be Obeyed says I'm nearly 40 in dog years (Her birthday's March 7th so She says I was special Birthday pressie – but She much much older than me)"

3. Does yoo have any brofurs or sisfurs?

"I have a Big Bossy Brother called Pilot – he a spanl too but alpha dog & he can be very scary. Sometimes he gives me the evil eye and I freeze. She wishes She could have same effect but I know She loves me & I'm not so sure about Pilot.I also have a 'new' baby spanl Brother called Jaunty. He my Understudy and looks up to me for advice & help – most of which I give cos I'm a kind dog. I also have lots of other anipals family – 2 cats, 2 'orses, 40 funny bird things that I'm always havin to put back in their place – She calls 'em ducks 'n chickens but I call them peskies – and then there's lots of curly coated piggies who are great fun and let me play with them."

4. Who does u live wiv?

"I live in a house with The Big Boss and She Who Must be Obeyed – they my People"

5. What is it like bein a workin dog and what kind of things do you do?

"It was hard work learnin' my job but I love it mostest of all even more than eatin (which is my next favouritest thing) and wish I could work every day but it's only 4 months each year. My main job is bush beatin' which means I have to hunt out all the pesky birds and babbits that hide in the undergrowth wherever She tells me to go. I go bish, bash, bosh, ping em out.... It might be under hedges & bushes, kale & maize, bogs & briars or the thickest bramble woods you ever did see. It's the excitingest thing in all the world. I'm Bestestgundog cos I'm steady & listen to her whistles & words & watches her hand signals - most of the time, though she says now I getting 'too clever for my own paws' – whatever that means – and don't listen so well! (Well – I knows better than Her where all the birds are – I have a very good nose and She can smell nothin' not even

if She fall over it!). Imagine a whole week's walks in one day! It very tiring but I never want to stop & quite often don't want to get in car to come home at end of day.

I also get asked to find lost birds that other dogs can't find cos of my xtra good nose & that can be very hard work cos the other dogs mess up all the good smells & makes the ground mucky with their scent. I've done plain pickin up too – which is findin the birds the guns shoot straight after they shot them ..that easy peasey. Sometimes tho the guns don't know what they shot and where it went and that make it much more interesting – tho then they say I stupid if I don't find the birds...... sometimes there were no birds... they stupid..."

6. Does you enjoy bein a workin dog and does yoo get paid?

"I loves bein a workin dog more than anythin'. Everybody say I'm like a computer – I have stand-by mode between 'drives' (that's what we call the huntin' bits) – and then go into turbo mode when I start huntin again. I get paid lots of compliment and cuddles and always get more food during shooting season. When it's not shootin season I don't really work 'cept at my lessons and at keepin piglets under control – but that's not the same thing at all. S'pose I'm gonna have a bit of work to do with bringin up the Understudy if he's gonna come out with us next Season..."

7. Why did yoo join Twitter?

"I'm a friendly sort of chap & wanted to get in touch with other spanls cos Pilot not very friendly to me so I can't woof much with him – 'cept on his terms (which are very strict). I wanted to know what other spanl's lives were like compared with mine cos I don't know much about other lives."

8. What does yoo enjoy most about bein on Twitter?

"I loves it most when my funny pals do funny things and makes Her laugh too – and we love the Croonin canine – you so clever Harry. P'raps we like bein a little bit nosey too?"

9. Does you fink dat Twitter is good fur do if so why?

"I think it's good cos how else would we all woof with each other and learn what else is goin on in the world – no two lives are the same and there's so much to woof about and sometimes if you havin a bad day and you go Twitterin you find one of your pals has done a funny thing or you find a pal who's sad and you realise your life not so bad. Mind you – The Big Boss say we twitter too much and sometimes it keeps us 'wake at night! But then, so does Pilot... and lots of other things come to think of it......."

Uncle Sandy
@SandyBridgend

He is a wuvly hoomin who praises us when good and guides us when norty BOL He wuvs his planes which is why he uses de picfur above on twitter.

1. Hi Uncle Sandy how's u doin?

"Hello Nephew Harry. As you know I is not too good just now. Just been diagnosed with Chronic Fibromyalgia. That is very sore in all my muscles/ligaments all the way through my body and has Chronic Diabetic Neuropathy all the way through my body too. I has two rythym problems with my heart. Atrial Fibrillation and Super Ventricular Tachycardia. (SVT For Short). I has Type 2 Diabetes. Menieres Syndrome (means I cannot fly) and a few other problems as well, so, I am not a happy bunny just now."

2. Is yoo young or old in dog years?

"If a Dog year is 7 Human years Then I is 7 Dog years + 2 Human Years = 51.. Still a Spring Chicken...... lol (Sometimes Feels Young, Most of the time Feels Old)"

3.   Who does u live wiv?

"I lives with my Brufur Martin. He is my Registered Carer now and helps me get on with daily life. I also lives with my Best Pal "Lucy-Lou" (Lucy for short) She is a ten yr old Cross Lab-Lurcher and I loves her too bits."

4.   Why did u join Twitter?

"As my illness got worse I googled for friend sites on the web and Twitter came up so I decided to give it a try. I was getting lonely.. The place where I live is full of OAP's and peoples who works all day, so, I has no friends here to speak too. I needed communication to keeps my brain stimulated."

5.   What does u enjoy most about bein on Twitter?

"I Has made many new friends on Twitter and also been able to communicate with people in the industry I worked in. A lot of people that I do not really know have shown me care and compassion and are showing to be good friends who look out for me and I enjoys speaking with my anipals too."

6.   Does u fink Twitter is a good fing fur dogs and hoomins if so why?

"I does think it is a good thing. It is a good thing for me anyway as I has loved dogs all my life and sometimes trusts them and their owners a lot more than other Humans. I finds it easy to relate to dogs."

7.   Does u tweet wiv any ofur anipals on Twitter is yes what kind?

I communicates with Alfie (Beardie) and his mum a lot.

Benjy the black bomber (dog) sometimes. Mardy the cat. Thomas Archer (dog) Winnie the pup (Dog training to be dog for the blind). I talks to various owners of other anipals.."

4

A TYPICAL DAY OR TWO

As well as Twitter I does lots of ofur fings wiv my day. So you will knows what I does I has done a diary of a typical day or two fur you to wead.

Thursday 25th October 2012

05:00 I got wudely awoken by my hoomin dis morning wanting to takes me into da garden fur a pee pee. My hoomins has not wealised as yet dat jus because dey is up at dawns crack dat does not mean dat I has to be! (appawently she couldn't sleep)

05:10 Back in my bed after bein slung out in da garden wiv hoomin sayin "pee pee do pee pee" like she insane. I didn't need a pee pee but I squatted and pwetended yoo know like u does jus to shut dem up BOL (yes I is a boy and yes I does squat to pee sometimes)

07:00 Back out of bed and out fur a walk up de lane wiv hoomin and Maggie my sisfur. I is on head halti so I not pull as I jus had a leg opewation in September. I hate my head halti and I push my head along de grass when I gets de opportunity on de field.

07:30 Bweakfast which is kibble and a bit of meat. If I lucky I get some veg and an egg sometimes.

07:30 and 20secs Finished bweakfast

07:31 Checkin out what hoomins havin fur bweakfast.

07:32 shouted at fur tryin to steal toast so gone to bed fur snooze.

08:00 in de garden havin a walk around and planning my day.

08:30 Had play fight wiv Maggie. She hangs off my ears! We got a bit carried away and I body slammed her and she yelped. Got shouted at again!

08:35 hoomin is in de utility woom sortin out de washin. I has managed to sneak out a pair of knickers and a sock BOL.

08:36 In my bed wiv hoomins knickers and a sock BOL

08:39 Hoomin in my woom and took de knickers and sock away fwom me. Got shouted at again BOL.

09:00 Havin a fink about why Auntie Bean not made any powidge yet on Twitter.

09:52 Auntie Bean asks us all on Twitter if any of us wants powidge.

10:11 I Tweets Auntie Bean to say I not allowed any cos I had my bweakfast. She a bit late in de day weally!

10:19 Auntie Bean says she will make me powidge tomorrow. I asks her if she has any wequests fur a song later.

10:21 Auntie Bean wequests Georgia on my mind but says I can subtute Summer fur Georgia.

11:02 Humf offers to play song on geeeeetar later.

11:04 Auntie Bean says it would be better on de peano so Humf agwees and I say I wills count him in.

11:05 Out fur walk agin up de lane. I only allowed a few lead walks a day until my leg heals.

11:30 Back home got a tweat of a biscuit vewy nice.

11:35 In de garden wiv Maggie. She wanderin around sniffin fings. I wonder if I should do some gardening. Yes I should.

11:40 I has gathered some leaves and some sticks so fur and put dem in my bed. I is now collecting some plants too which are nice and muddy at de bottom.

11:45 I has started to design my inside garden wiv an array of house plants.

11:50 Hoomin has come into me bedwoom and seen my changing woom design. I was quite impwessed by what I has achieved but she not. I no understand as dey have house plants so why I can't do de same. Needless to say……..got shouted at BOL

12:00 Giving up on being norty so gonna have a snooze.

13:00 Check Twitter account. Nuffin happenin.

13:30 Thought of my wuv Summer and wondered what she doin. Started to pwactice my song fur her.

14:00 Went to check de garden to make sure it still der.

14:20 Had anofur play fight wiv Maggie. No-one gots hurt dis time.

14:45 Hoomins goin out fur some weason wivout us.

14:50 Sat by door fur 5 minutes listenin to see if hoomins outside but Maggie say dey gone out in da car.

15:00 Had play fight wiv Maggie and now sat by de French doors lookin in de garden growling at de pidgeons.

15:15 Pulled blankets off my bed and piled dem in de middle of de floor wiv Maggies help.

15:20 Took de cushions off de kitchen chairs and put dem on top of de blankets in my woom.

15:22 Havin a snooze wiv Maggie on de new bed we made fur eachofur.

16:00 Uh uh hoomins back and not impwessed wiv de bed we made but dey no shout.

16:02 out in da garden fur a pee.

16:05 Has me dinner which is kibble again.

16:05 and 20 secs Finnished dinner and now checkin to see if Maggie left any behind. She hasn't.

17:00 Out fur a walk on de field. Maggie off her lead I on mine.

17:05 Maggie sees a wabbit and runs after it. I has to walk as on de lead and hoomin no want to be dwagged along de gwass today like yesterday.

17:30 Back home.

18:00 Checkin out what hoomins havin for der dinner. Smells good and looks nicer dan mine!

19:50 Summer, de wuv of my life, tweets me to say she at de farm as her hoomins goin away on hollibobs wivout dem. She say she cwied a lot when dey left.

20:00 go to count Humf in on Twitter to do de song fur summer and Aunite Bean but Humf dispersed and he playin de peeeano. Slight panic.

20:13 Humf finally appears sayin he was tunin his peeano. I counts him in. We sing de song fur Summer and Auntie Bean.

20:24 song done and we all agwee dat we should call Simon Howl and ask fur a wecord deal.

20:25 Bestest Gun Dog Gunner complains dat he missed our song. I say sowwy.

21:48 Summer tweets us all to say she goin to bed. I say goodnight my luf and tell her I wuv her.

21:51 A nice hooman lady on Twitter asks how my day has been. She vewy polite to me.

22:02 I has a quick chat wiv Uncle Sandy.

22:10 I has pee pee and gets put to my bed. I gets kisses fwom both hoomans and 3 small sweeties and a cuddle.

22:11 zzzzzzzzzzzzzzzzzzzzzzzzzzzzzzzzzzzzzzzzzzz

Tuesday 20 November 2012

06:34 Not sure if it is day or night it is dat dark outside. De wain has bin hammerin all night and I as ardly slept.

06:36 Stare at Maggie, she is sleeping on the breakfast bar bench on a blanket. She is snoring her head orf as usual. I still confoosed dat somefin so small can make so much noise!

06:52 bored now so decide to wake de hoomins up BOL

06:53 WOOF WOOF WOOF WOOF WOOF WOOF WOOF WOOF......WOOF.......WOOF...WOOF....WOOF....WOOF

06:54 Giggle to myself cos I know de timed woofs dwive dem nuts hee hee hee.

06:56 hear footsteps job done

06:57 wun back to my bed and lie down so dey confoosed when de open de door.

06:57 and 20 seconds laugh at Maggie as she leaps orf de bweakfast bench and to her bed cos she no sure if she should be on it or not. She slides acwoss de floor loses her gwip and crashes into de chair BOL BOL BOL

06:57 and 30 seconds Boss mum comes in and asks what all de noise is about (stoopid question weally)

07:00 second in command aka mama comes in and dey start to put on wet weather gear. It blowin gale outside is dey mad!!!!!!!!

07:02 standin outside. Ears flappin up and down in de wind and de wain lashin all awound. Maggie twyin to walk wiv her eyes shut BOL

07:04 Maggie trips up second in command cos she still gots her eyes shut BOL

07:05 avin a poo. Wind whippin me bad legs ears flappin.

07:05 and 5 seconds still avin a poo but doin the poo walk to twy and chase de leaves at same time.

07:06 finish poo and got de leaves. Does victory poo dance which is scrapin legs behind me on de gwass likes I twyin to cover de poo BOL.

07:12 Maggie avin a poo she walks in circles and poos at de same time, dwives hoomins mad BOL

07:13 Walk back to house soaked through hoomins dwy in der wet weather gear though!

07:20 in house got towel dwied.

07:30 avin bweakfast

07:30 and 20 seconds finished bweakfast

07:31 checkin if Maggie got anyfing left in her bowl.......nope

08:00 avin a lie down check twitter account and see I has missed some messages fwom my wiv @summerhollett

08:30 hoomin second in command furiously cleanin de kitchen

09:30 fink about how nice it is to live in Devonia

10:30 Boss mum decides to take me and Maggie out in da wain again!!!!!! She has seriously got issues!

10:31 we got wain coats on dis time and Maggie orf lead she still has her eyes shut though.

10:34 Maggie runs orf oh uh she gonna be in big twouble

10:34 Boss mum shoutin and wislin fur Maggie but she disapeered.

10:35 Boss mum still shoutin we both gettin soaked standin in da wain. I decide to sit down and sit in big puddle which is cold and stand up stwaight away cos me bum shave after me op BOL

10:39 Maggie comes back and gets told orf big time by Boss mum. Maggie is all wet and muddy. Dis no good as yesterday she rolled in lots of poo when orf lead and went fwom black dog to brown dog as if by magic!

10:45 back in da house and Maggie sent to her bed. I get confoosed and go to bed too but Boss mum says no I bin good and calls me out of bed. Maggie comes too and Boss mum says "go to bed" I get confoosed and go to bed too but Boss mum says no I bin good and calls me out of bed Maggie comes too Boss mum say "go to bed" I get confoosed and go to bed......... you get de idea of wot was appenin BOL BOL BOL

10:46 Boss mum gives up and second in command twyin not to laugh

11:00 Boss mum in her office workin (at least dat wot she say she doin)

12:00 I visit Boss mum in de office to say hello. She kisses my head and tickles me ears

12:30 Second in command calls Boss mum fur somefin to eat. Dey must av skipped bweakfast dis morning cos I coulds not smell anyfing.

12:32 twy to grab some bacon orf de plate but cone gets in de way

12:33 lick de air near de plate it tastes so good nom nom nom

13:00 Boss mum says to come and she holdin me lead in her hand so I goes ofur to her. She no take me outside she take me into her office where de wet woom is.

13:03 I is confoosed and den I hear brrrrrrrrrrrrrr noise and see dat Boss mum has purchased some clippers!!!!!!!! *gulp*

13:04 Boss mum appwoaches me wiv de clippers

13:04 and 5 seconds I back away fwom Boss Mum

13:04 and 30 seconds Boss mum sayin what a good boy I am as if dat gonna make a difference when she gots those fings in her hand!

13:04 and 50 seconds I wun out of lead and Boss mum is on me wiv de clippers

background info now I don't mind being groomed I quites likesit weally when it is done by de pwoffessionals but.... Mu hoomin is no pwoffessional gwoomer. Now I wecently had two operwations and as part of deses operwations I got me back leags and bum shaved so I am quite keen to hang on to whatefur fur I has left.

13:06 I can see me fur fallin on the gwound and in a blind panic I start to gather it up de best I can.

13:07 in an attempt to stop de torture I lie down and roll on me back.

13:08 Boss mum makes me stand up

13:09 I lie down

13:10 Boss mum makes me stand up

13:11 I lie down

13:12 Boss mum starts on me ears and as a wesult I has one ear shorter dan de ofur cos I kept lien down on one side!

13:15 escape and head fur back door

13:17 Second in command takes us out

14:00 Me and Maggie get given a tweat of a hoof stuffed full of nice tasty stuff

15:00 still enjoyin my tweat and wealise I has not had me cone on since after de bacon incident woo hoo

17:00 Boss mum takes away tweat and gives us our dinner

17:00 and 20 seconds finish dinner and starin at Maggie. Der was a time when I would stare and she would give me her food but dat no work anymore but still worth a twy

18:00 On Twitter talkin to me pals

19:00 out fur quick walk

19:25 talkin to pals on twitter I does wuv dem all vewy much. Auntie Bean gives us all sossige. I swap my chilli one fur a beef one as I not want a wunny bum BOL BOL

20:00 sleepin on sofa. Has nicked second in commands space so she sittin on de dog blanket side BOL BOL BOL

21:00 orf out fur last walk we can hear lots of owls hootin loudly

22.00 in my bed has 3 tweats and cuddles

22.01 and 30 seconds
zzzzzzzzzzzzzzzzzzzzzzzzzzzzzzzzzzzzzzzzzzzzzzzzzzzzz
zzzzzzzzzzzzzzzz

5

TENNIS BALLS – MY EXPERIENCES

I luv tennis balls I can't hide it. All types of tennis balls fwom de cheap to de expensive (although de cheap ones don'ts last as long as de expensive ones and don't bounce as high)

Now I can sniff a tennis ball out a mile away. It's twue, I can lose one of my tennis balls and find it a year later even if it is covered in moss. Pwetty cool eh! I has also twied an experience wiv my tennis balls which my hoomans buy in box loads fwom a well known on-line auction site! I has put my tennis balls down wabbit holes to see what would appen. Well I can weport dat dis is de quickest way to lose your tennis balls fur good and is not weckommended by me at all. Howefur, I has had two balls weturned by de babbits as dey pushed dem out der babbit hole but dat is a 2 in 50 chance of any weturn so do not do.

I can hold two tennis balls in my mouf at de same time! My hooman say it cos I got a big mouf, how wude, I say it cos I is so vewy vewy clever! I did not always get de joy of tennis balls I must admit. I nefur used to be able to catch de tennis bals when my hoomans threw dem fur me. De use to hit me wight between de eyes and bounce orf BOL BOL. It took me a while to get de hang of de fact dat I was supposed to catch de ball and not dat my hoomans where jus throwing fings AT me for fun! BOL
I soon gots de hang of it and has not looked back since.

My hoomans get as excited as me when de new tennis balls

awwive. Dey show me de box and I spin round and round and den dey open de box and tips all de balls on de floor at once. I get so excited and chase all de balls around. Dat is how I learned to pick up two at a time. I am currently working on picking up three at once.

Here are some picfurs of me wiv my tennis balls:

Even when asleep I want me tennis balls! (Though mum takes them orf me in case I chokes)

Dis is a tennis ball hatchery I came acwoss on a walk! All de tennis balls where on de sticks but I could nots get in!

I has jus wecently moved house to Devonia. I was not entirely appy wiv movin as I now got to makes me mark again. Howefur, once I gots to new house guess what is next to my garden...................a tennis court wiv lots of tennis balls. So I has now gots my own position fur when de balls escape I will catch dem and dey will be mine!

6

IT WASN'T ME

So how many times has u bin blamed fur somefin dat was not ur fault? I weckon us dogs gets blamed fur loads and loads. De classic one is dat pawful smell in de woom. You know de one dat de hooman blames on you. Gwanted sometimes it is us but not always. So when dey go "oh Harry you stink" when in fact it is weally dem dat has let some hideous wind escape fwom der bottom what is a dog to do? It is not as if we can say no it wasn't!

So de ofur day I had been blamed one time too many so I came up wiv a plan to gets me own back. You see dey had guests dat day and dey bwought me pal Harv wiv dem. Harv is a shitzoo and has de tendency to let rip de most howendous smell fwom his tiny bum. I kid you not it is foul I has never known such a tiny dog to make such a stinky pong. Harv is quite pwoud of dis and lets rip at wills. So de plan was formed. Maggie, Harv and me sat ourselves in specific places in de sitting woom. Maggie was on de sofa wiv boss hooman and Auntie Michelle Harvs humum, I was sat as far away fwom my hoomans as possible and Harv was sat wiv his hudad Wussell so we ad formed a twiangle. Well the sucker fur dis evenings fun game of "it wasn't me" was mama who was sat on de sofa on her own.

So at a stwategic moment I started twyin to lick my scar which acted as a distwaction. At de point when efuryone was lookin at me Harv snuck ofur to de side of de sofa and let rip den snuck back and layed down agin pwetendin to be asleep. Well....... Mama said "yuk dat disgustin smell" and covered her nose wiv her jumper. But de ofur hoomans could not smell Harvs hideous smell cos dey were not sat where mama was so de ofur hoomans started to tease mama sayin it must be her cause no-one else near her not even de dogs BOL BOL. No matter how much mama pwotested dey still said it must be her! Oh how we all giggled as our plan ad worked. Dat will teach her!

When der is more dan one anipal in de house it is welatively easy to use de line "It wasn't me" particularly if you has younger anipals as furblings. My sisfur Maggie likes to copy me sometimes particularly if she gets weally excited and cawwied away and furgets dat what she is doin is norty. As I is older I is quicker to look innocent and discard any bwanches, soil or ofur garden fings I has bin chewing. Howefur Maggie is jus not dat quick which works to my advantage. She has bin blamed fur fings like chewing sticks in de house, bwinging leaves in, spilling water efurywhere and putting mud on de carpet. She was also nearly blamed fur making a mess in our woom. Now u may fink I is cwuel fur dis but wemember she hangs fwom my ears, body slams me and nicks me tennis balls. All is fur in wuv and war and as I has said befur it is a dog eat dog world!

Here are some of de fings dat I has done but I will say "it wasn't me"

I twied to blame Maggie fur dis but she small and hoomans said she could not pull de pillows so I got busted.

Harry the Spaniel

Dis is a simple case of dog and hoomin miscommunications. You see dey said I makes a mess I say "it wasn't me" den I wealise dat dey meant my indoor garden was de mess dey was weferring to! How wude!

If you fail to come up wiv excuses twy to hide. Can you see me? BOL

Dis is me bein accused of nickin me mums slippers…….well ok

caught wed pawed dey suits me dough don'ts dey?

So to sum up if yoo do somfin but want to get out of twouble here are some tips;

1) Blame your sisfur or brofur but make sure de cwime is one dat is capable of bein committed by dem.

2) if der are hoomin children in de house particularly babies twy blamin de messes on dem. Dat is fair given dey puuls ur ears etc.

3) Pwactice ur innocent face at least 5 time a week so dat it comes naturally when needed.

4) pwetend to feel sick dat is a sure way of casuin a distraction. Cough like yoo has somefin stuck in ur throat and watch dem panic. Any nortiness will soon be furgotten.

5) Be somewhere else when de nortiness is discovered.

6) RUN

7

MY LAST THOUGHTS

So yoo has made it to the end of my furst book. Well done. I hopes dat der are some good tips in here fur you to follow.

Fur yoo hoomins out der us dogs is a simple creature. We are highly intelligent (more so dan you lot) and spend most of our time twainin you when you fink you are twaining us! Treat us kindly and wuv us efury day and we will stick to you like glue. We will wuv you back unconditionally (well apart fwom food and tweats) We ask fur no more dan dat fwom yoo.

Fur my fellow canines, continue in ur quest to be norty. It does make de hoomins laugh secwetly and gives dem somfin interesting to talk about. Continue to sniff bums, eat horse poo, make indoor gardens and all de ofur cwazy fings we like to do. Enjoy your lives and be happy and content.

Whilst der are lots of fings in dis cwazy world I does not understand and whilst hoomins does fings dat are just totally insane, I does wuv my life and my family both with fur and without. I wuv my pals on twitter and de many fings dey get up to.

So, enjoy life, embwace it and I will meets you all again in my next book.

Fur now dis is Harry de Spaniel pawing orf.

xxxxxxx

8

DICTIONARY FUR HOOMANS

5 Bones – 5 star rating of hotels

agweed – agreed

Anipals – Animals

bedwoom – bedroom

betfur – better

Bin – been

BMAO – Bark my arse off (Laugh my arse off)

BOL – Bark out Loud (Laugh out loud)

brofur – brother of de anipal kind

Bweakfast – breakfast

celebwate – celebrate

Cofur – cover

Confoosin – confusing

Crooning Canine – Dats me dat is I is de crooning canine

Cwied – cried

Dat - That

Dem – Them

Der – There or their

Dey – They

Dog and Bone – Phone

Doin - Doing

Eachofur – each other

Eaten – eating

fanks – thanks

Fing – thing

Fink – think

Fought – thought

Foughtful – Thoughtful

fud – food

Fur – For

Fur de wuv of dog – for the love of God

Furever – forever

Fweind – friend

Fwom – from

Gawgus - Gorgeous

Gweat – great

Gweif – grief

hallow – hello

Harmonia – harmonica

Hawwy – Harry

hoomans – humans

hoomins – humans

IBone – IPhone

ill – I'll

IPawd – IPad

Mus – must

Norty – Naughty

OMD – Oh my dog (Oh my God)

paw – foot or poor

pawfect – perfect

pawsom – awesome

pawty – party

Peano - Piano

peeps – people

Pet hotel – kennel

Picfur – picture

Powidge – porridge

Puddle – puddle or muddle

Pwecisely – precisely

Pwison – prison

Pwobably – probably

Pwoof – proof

ROTFB – Roll on the floor Barking (Roll on the floor laughing)

sisfur – sister of the anipal kind

Sittin – sitting

Sossiges – Sausages

Spanbol – Spaniel

Spanner – Spaniel

Spwing – spring

stoopid – stupid

Swatchin – scratching

Togefur – together

twied – tried

twyin – trying

u – you

Unwequited – unrequited

urry – hurry

Vewy – very

Wadio - Radio

Wain – rain

Weally – really

weception – reception

wiv – with

woom – room

Wot – what

wude – rude

Wuvly – lovely

Xtwa – extra

Der are plenty more wurds dat we use on Twitter u will have to learn as u go along.

ABOUT THE AUTHOR

Harry Wilson Nesbitt-Collins is an English Springer Spaniel born January 2010 in Essex. He has one sisfur called Maggie who is a rescue dog. He lives with his hoomans in Devon where he moved to from Essex. He enjoys being out on the field, swimming and chasing tennis balls and rabbits. He has recently had two operations on both his back legs after he ruptured both cruciate ligaments within weeks of each other. Harry takes most things in his stride but does not like the hose, car or roads. He is much loved by his hooman parents and sisfur.

ABOUT THE CO-AUTHOR

Heather Nesbitt was born in N.Ireland and lives with her partner Yvonne and their two dogs Harry and Maggie in Devon. Heather runs her own company and this book started out as a hobby whilst she was ill and in recovery. She enjoys walking and reading and tweeting for Harry and her company.

Printed in Great Britain
by Amazon.co.uk, Ltd.,
Marston Gate.